Poems of Love and Pain

The Collected Poetry of David Donald White
2016-2025

David sometimes writes under the pseudonyms No-One, The Young-Red-Shadow-Dragon and Slow-Hand

David Donald White

Dedicated to Paige Becker, Sharon Muz, Philip Muz and Mark Muz

Special thanks to Mark Elliott Muz, the cover artist

Copyright © 2025 by David Donald White

Contents

Shadows of Delight 2

Boxcars in the Sky 3

Life 4

Gone 6

'67 Beaumont 7

An Ode to Bad Poetry 9

Toulouse 11

Hemingway 12

Chasing Ghosts 14

Burnt Out 17

Love Poem 19

The Ashes 20

Moral Relativism 22

Dispatches from Wuhan 24

Counterfeit Cowboy 27

TUMS 28

Anywhere 29

Blood on the Blacktop 30

The Violence and the Rage	33
The Dance	34
Ashes to Ashes	35
The Bad and Ugly and The Beautiful - A Poem About Bipolar	36
Courage	38
My Cat Mars	39
Glass Eye	40
The Wolf and the Poet	43
The Night Writer	46
Alone	47
Strawberry	48
Searching for Woody Guthrie	49
A Hundred Miles from Home	51
Five Years	52
Loss	53
The Bronze Age Collapse	54
Orphan's Cry	56
Block 1912 in the Late Summer	58
Minerva	60
The Hero's Journey	61
Near the Ashes: A Saskatchewanian Odessey	66
The Siren of Saskatchewan	67
The Solstice and the Strawberry Moon	68
Close Your Eyes	71

In Her Absence 73
The Harrowing of the Heiros Gamos or As I Fade Away 75
The Wreckage 76
Minerva's Man 78
Prairie Colossus 79
The Tournament 80
Home 81
Your Heart Warms Me 82
Surrender 83
Manic Depression 84
Shark Week 86
First, You Must Love Yourself 87
Drunken Nights 88
The Oak and the Ash 89
Madness Sweet Madness 90
Wild Albertan Sky 91
Under a Blue Moon 93
Never Use the Word Love in a Poem 94
Circles in Cycles 96
The Harsh Light of Day 97
Doing Time in the COVID Hotel 98
Prairie Girl 100
The Tragedy of Our Malady 101
Inevitable as Rain 103

In my Haunting Dreams 104

Sad Songs 106

Ithaca 108

Father 109

The Search for Meaning 110

The Aviary 112

Dreams 114

Smoldering Auburn 115

Midnight Driver 116

In the Throes of Thanatos (The Death Instinct) 118

Burning 119

Through Those Pines 120

The Inverted Tree 122

As the Starlight Fades 123

Let Go 125

The Moon and the Ocean Tide 126

Shadows of Delight

I've lived a thousand years
Dreams of lives
echo in the marrow
of my bones
Whispers of realities I've wished for
Or feared in the silence of the darkness

I've fought great dragons
With sword lifted high
Charging into the fire
Relishing the fear

I've spent a life
with a woman I've never met
Who nursed my wounds
And loved me with passion
In the halls of my keep

Boxcars in the Sky

Lightning strikes in the night

The flash of the light

The far-off thunder rumble

The moonlight on the pond

Rippled and distorted by the roar

Life

A symphony of pieces moving together

Notes of Darkness and light,

joy and pain

We live and we lie through it,

When the symphony plays our death note

Well, then we die to it

But in between we have choices

Who to love and who to hate

What to stand up for and when to be late

Where to lay low and how to disappear

One day we noticed we've grown old

Laugh lines or frown

wrinkles all the same

The universe doesn't care

If you had a good time

Or struggled your way though

Whether you gave your life meaning

Or just refused to understand

The magic of life is so easily ignored

One thing you'll realize on your death bed

It was all up to you

Gone

My darlin' I swore that I loved you
And you swore to be true
But I'm sitting here
and I don't know who you are

Gone and done by
The time flies
I wish you would
have told me why

Maybe I'll never know
Why you chose to go
But I been feeling real low
As the cold winds blow

'67 Beaumont

She's got 53 years of sweat
and knuckle blood and rust in her guts

Her panels swell like a woman's hips,
the metal bulging and muscular,
but undeniably feminine.

She's seen hundreds
of thousands of miles,
so many that the odometer
can't even count
how far she's gone.
Her ancient wheels
showing the same patina
that she does.

A car from the summer of love.

The sail panels extending far past

 and buttressing the rear windshield

They don't build 'em like this anymore

An Ode to Bad Poetry

You broke my heart

Ripped the viscera

from the ballrooms of my chest

Loaded up and headed west

But darlin' I'm tougher than that

If that's your best

Darlin' I know you're hurting

I can hear it in your voice

You lash out at me

With that sharp cutting tongue

And say I meant nothin' to you

But darlin' I'm tougher than that

I still dream of you

but I get no rest

Now years have passed us by

Marriages come and gone

I wrote you bad poetry

And you wrote Bad Poetry

Found at the bottom

of your bottle of gin

Like a bad joke I'm a mess

But darlin' I'm tougher than that

If that's your best

Toulouse

He smells of old leather

The fragrance of wine

And the spice of cigarette smoke

I breathe deep

The bravado

And bad mustaches

At once masculine

And sensitive

A pacifist

A brother

in a farewell

To arms

Hemingway

Self-annihilation

The death instinct

Numb feelings

And self-medication

Destructive decisions

The mortal struggle with hopelessness

The comfortable dark

Life doesn't end like this

But the very attempt to live

The beautiful and the ugly

The truth in the bottom of the bottle

And the word on the page

The writers only refuge

The lead loaded in the gun

The cordite smell

He's gone now

Splattered on the wall

And the damage is done

He was only sixty-one

Chasing Ghosts

Looking into your eyes

Mirrors of mine

Your heart

so passionate and sad

And beautiful and sweet

I held it once

In my broken hands

Kept it near

My broken heart

You loved me truly

And unconditionally

I loved you

As well as I could

But I wasn't there

Out chasing ghosts

and demons and shadows

While you kept the porch light lit

That's my curse, to chase ghosts

While the woman I love grows cold

Alone

As the porch light burns low

And dies

Now I'm alone

Full of regret

Now the ghost is you

And I chase you

Every night in my dreams

But you're long gone

You were my soul mate

And I can only hope

That when were both dead and gone

I might get another chance to love you

Properly this time

Memories washed away

Echoes of this life

Sounding in our souls,

together at last

In heaven or the next life

Forever my wife

Burnt Out

That feeling in your gut
When you wonder
if you're the only living soul

That thought in your mind
When there's nothing left to write
And the darkness creeps in

And you wonder if it's all worthwhile
And you think to yourself and smile
They'd never miss me for long

And you flick your cigarette
to the pavement
And crush it with your sole

But you think you
couldn't care less
If you burnt it all down

The fire in your heart

smoldered out years ago

But once in a while

The embers get kicked up

And glow red once again

If only for a fleeting moment

And so, you go on

Waiting to feel something

once again

To burn again

Love Poem

You would never have your sweet name roll from my lips, gagged and sullen

And you would never have me write to you in a moment of weakness so sweet so

Yet every word I've written whispers your name

On every page a painting of your effervescent face

And the quickening of my heartbeat at the thought of you

I wish I could escape the memory of you

But without the memories

I would have lost the love I felt for you

If not the love perhaps the loss of love to fall

But if not you, then who?

The Ashes

The slits of sunlight

Stab like jagged little knives

Eyes burst open

Thirst like smoke

Swells the tongue

Quenched

as the ashes run down

his face

Bitter taste

From the cigar

the night before

Gives way

To cleansing

Water

It runs down his back

As he washes the sweat

And the stench

of the club

Away

Moral Relativism

We suffer in this life

We never fucking asked for it

But we do what we must to survive

We do what we must to get by

Our grandfathers knew evil

And gladly died fighting it

Evil is more insidious now

Right and wrong

The battle lines aren't clear

We live in no man's land now

Where the truth is subjective

The worst of us make the most sense

And the rest are full of contradictions and hypocrisy

We long for a moral compass

As we struggle

and fumble fuck around

In the darkness

Dispatches from Wuhan

Another day

59 more

The doctor's on the radio

It's a quarter to four

Two more deaths

21,000 so far

Bend the curve they say

Locked up in isolation

For months or more we stay

The children out of school

But the playgrounds are empty

Social distancing is the rule

Where once there were plenty

The lucky amongst us work from home
The unfortunate are fired by the thousands
Our gas tanks are full
But we have nowhere to roam

Valiant workers stock the store shelves
And tireless truckers tires lay down long miles
Thankless professions in better times
now holding together, the social fabric of civil society
Putting aside their own safety
all to keep us fed
as the virus is spread

My generation was so flippant and sarcastic
We thought nothing and no one could touch us
Now no one can
We had no character defining societal trauma like The Great War
To toughen us up for the existential threat of our Spanish Flu

One day this will all be a memory

And one day our children will ask

where were we when the news of Wuhan broke

And we will be there to answer

Or so we hope

Counterfeit Cowboy

Don't ride no horse

Don't got no boots

Don't drive no Cadillac

But I've been to the hoosegow

For a night or two

Don't ride no rodeo

Don't chew no tobacco

Don't live in the country

But I wear an old Concho hat

And we can step outside

If you got a problem with that

TUMS

TUMS are delicious candy

For people with and without

Acid reflux

Anywhere

When you're gone
and I lay there
Wallowing in dark despair
With ache and weight in my heart
When slumber finally takes me

But in reality, you're never there
I can't find you anywhere
You've gone and moved on
But in my dreams, you're still there

Blood on the Blacktop

In the hazy sunset we run

Howling, big block Chevy's and Ford's

Pound their way down the pavement

Torque twisting the motor mounts

Engines shifting in the chassis from the power

White chalk on black asphalt

draws the battle lines

The ready lights come on

Prestaged then staged

Four eyes focused on the tree

Engines screaming like banshees

Two hearts racing

The lights begin to fall down the tree

Amber

Amber

Amber

Green

Lightning strikes the accelerator
In tenths of a second
The drive line shock
The power tears at the pavement
The rear sidewall twists on the bead
Warping the raised white letters

The nose becomes weightless
As the front tires lift off the ground
Eight cylinders burning and pulsing
Nine hundred horses of Detroit muscle

All you can see is sky
For a quarter of a mile
If you can stay in it

And the shoot rips

And your front wheels eat pavement

And if you're lucky you didn't blow your engine

And if you're lucky you see your rival in the mirror

And if you're really lucky you see only yourself

The Violence and the Rage

The revolution is coming

The drum beats louder now

Heard in the moans of the drug addicts in the streets

The tent colonies in the heart of every city

The Police can't clear them fast enough

The violence and the rage

The broken promise

and the opium plague

The tent cities

and the unrest is growing

while the rich get richer

oblivious to the struggle

The Dance

Life moves fast
People come and they go
I wish I could slow the music sometimes
To linger in the beauty of the tune
Sometimes I forget
In the monotony of it all
That I better wear my Sunday best
There are no second chances
And there will never be a second dance

Ashes to Ashes

A simple pine box

They wanted to be buried

Ashes in the dirt

The Bad and Ugly and The Beautiful - A Poem About Bipolar

The bad and ugly, and the beautiful

Life is a series of tragedies

It'll beat you down if it can

Or if you're weak

It takes strength to be vulnerable

But it also takes a fool

to expose their soft belly

too long to the knife of life

Entropy destroys everything

All the sandcastles we've built

Will be washed away with the ocean tide

It can tear apart even the strongest men

But there is beauty in the pain

Beauty in the sunset of the beach

The castle casts a shadow across the sand

Glistening in the sun

Before it is swept away

Moments caught in time

Never to be caught again

Some feel the tragedy intensely

Others are oblivious and content

For those that feel the pain of life

Down to the bone

Those moments of beauty

Must be captured somehow

Or that life

long or short

And all that pain

was in vain

Courage

Rushing into a fire

In the face of the fury

and the anger of the flames

My Cat Mars

The cat must've been crazy
But I loved him like a brother
Even though he pissed on my clothes
and made me smell like a mad cat man

But he was me
And I was him
And one day the world ended
behind my couch
He wanted to go alone
The little Conquistador of death

But we found him
And took him to the vet
And he drifted away on morphine
An ending not fit for his name
The God of war

Glass Eye

I used to think I was tough

Had been in a few small-town fights

Won once or twice

Always wanted to be

one of the tough guys

Hung at the rough bars

Drove some fast cars

Thought I could live forever

in invincible youth

Until one night I saw the truth

The bar was full

My companion and I walked in

Every step stuck to the filthy floor

We had barely made it through the door

15 feet away at the bar I hear shouting
My companion and I look over
To hear the sound of a bottle breaking

On the brass of the bar
On the down swing
it was upside down in his hand
round and hard, made to end fights

It is broken now
terrible and jagged
Made to mutilate
Its victim might have been 25
Maybe younger

The upswing brought
The mutilator into the victim's face
Cutting his handsome flesh
into red ribbons and lace
And his eye

The bystanders ran

and we were no different

As the bouncers disarmed the assailant

Too late that night boys

I remember the shock

and the vomit outside

And the quiet drive home

And the screaming in my mind

I saw the victim about a year later

His mutilated face was hard to look away from

But also, hard to look at

I didn't wanna be a tough guy after that

His glass eye looked right through me

The Wolf and the Poet

His smile was crooked

There was a darkness in it

I could feel it in my soul

As the stranger lit a match

Breathed that hot tobacco in deep

The wind whistled

like a thousand widows cries

"I hear you want to make a deal"

Leaning up against the wall

His wolf smile flashed into a wolf grin

As he took another draw

"Maybe you want to be a folk singer,

Or to live on the silver screen

Or to ride the bulls in the big rodeos?"

"I can give you more money than you could ever spend. A woman you would love beyond belief. You could author the most beautiful works of art man and woman has ever seen. Your name would echo through the years like Hank WIlliams or Dylan Thomas, Bob Dylan even"

He knew my next question before the words formed on my lips

"The price I exact will hurt you, or those around you more than you'll ever know,

Maybe you'll die at 27, the tragedy haunting your name and memory, always known for who you could have been, what you could have written."

"Or maybe the woman I introduced you to, the mother of your future children, will die in a car accident, tragedy will run through your gains as long as you live, the balance must be restored, if I fix things in your favor for a time, but who knows, you may get lucky and die of old age surrounded by loved ones…"

I thought long and hard about it

A few cold moments passed

then he smiled again.

The Night Writer

When the day is done
And you're done bleeding
You stumble home
in the darkness
A pointless struggle

As you open up your veins again
And bleed your heart's blood
onto the page
So full of gutless rage
Restless and wrecked

Acclaim here and gone
Fleeting it dances
In flashes and glances

Alone

I've been alone

Burnt down to the ground

The Wood and ash

Coat my lungs

But I shall never die

Life grows even as the trees lie

Eternal as the sun

Ageless as the flood

That carved the rocks

That cut the world

That washed it clean

Strawberry

In the night her visage comes to me

She's as I longed her to be

Strawberry blonde in her hair

Forlorn for years

I lay there

I whispered I love you

And in my dreams

she'd say it too

Searching for Woody Guthrie

Searching deep within

Looking for old Woody Guthrie

With his machine

Made to kill fascists

With a chord and a word

He could put them down like dogs

Searching deep within

Looking for young Phil Ochs

The Broadside Balladeer

His lyrics cut the establishment

Down to the bone

So the FBI hounded him

And choked him to death

With his own hand

Searching deep within

Looking for young Bobby Dylan

The greatest songwriter who ever lived

Writing America a conscience

one song at a time

But I ain't no song writer

Ain't got no fire in my belly

against the establishment

And I ended no fascists

with my words

My poetry is too soft

For these angry political days

Am I part of the problem

For not raging against

the injustices of life

What have I got to say

At the end of the day

A Hundred Miles from Home

When the sun goes down
The last light slowly dies
Rays of pink and orange and blues
Over the sun spun yellow wheat

The last moments of day
Fading over the bales of hay
The Canadian prairies
The American West
A bygone day gone away

The land of legends
The last frontier
A dusty country road
Only a hundred miles from home

Five Years

Her hair glistened in the mid-day sun
I longed to be with her, for us to be one
Once there were two, now there are none

oh, how I loved you
down to the marrow of my bones
where the blood that burns for you is born
And oh, how it's burned for you
these five long years

It burns for you as I wake
And as I work the day through
In the night there is only you

Loss

Constantly navigating
The loss in my heart
Hard to be vulnerable
When it's broken into shards

Here and gone
Always alone
But I'm getting used to it
The Solitude
down to the bone

Haunted by the past
My demons burning in the night
Let them burn, I'll use the light

The Bronze Age Collapse

A time of Madness and rage

The gods went insane

and idols were smashed

They came from the sea

and slaughtered those

that did not flee

The apocalypse of the bronze age

The coming of the dark

even their language was lost

Stories of the ocean

Ships on the horizon

hulking frigates

full of fear

At Crete they ran for the hills

Hiding in the stone

At Knossos they ate their children

Butcher marks left on the young bone

Orphan's Cry

Beaten down Bloodied black and blue

Strength dawn from the bottom of an empty well

And crying cannot quell

The pain in this empty shell

But this ice might kill the swell

Walking down the highway with one shoe

Like we all do

Crying for our mothers in the grey moonlight

Weary but always ready for a fight

Just lost children running in the night

Sometimes I wonder where that shoe went

But then I start to limp

and the pain seeps back in

Best left forgotten

Like our destination

And the mothers

We howl alone

We all howl alone

Block 1912 in the Late Summer

Lights are strung

Across the ceiling

Hanging from wires

Books and abstract paintings

line the walls and halls

On old oak shelves

And earth tone paint

The sound of the street

And passers by

Wander in from the open facade

The writer sits alone

And writes a poem

in a shirt he made

With a plateau hat on

and a stalk of lavender

in the conchos of the band

The chrome of the coffee makers

Reflect the soft warm light from the ceiling

A couple is meeting for the first time

At the table behind him

Nervous laughs and blushing smiles

He feels a touch of envy at what lies ahead of them

An older couple sits

in high backed chairs

Too far away to talk

She looks content

to be in her own world

The tables begin to clear out

The light from the street is fading

And the air is getting colder

Soon fall will be here

And the facade will be closed

Minerva

Once a month she rises with the twilight

Dancing across the sky my muse and I

Her light so softly glows

upon the houses row on row

Lovers embrace in her radiance

Her moonlit face dances across the water

Its ripples could never detract

Or distract from her perfection

Oh, how I long for You

Have you waited for me too?

He asks, the question is not new

Could she be You? Is my waiting through?

Once or twice, he thought he knew

The Hero's Journey

The call echoed throughout the ages

The call to action

To take up the mantle

To seek adventure

My existence changed when I heard that call

Once a sleepwalker through life

with the fire burning weak

Turned way down low

She awoke it in me

Passion burnt like fire

dancing in the night

It burnt with a white-hot flame

For her

Only for her

A province away
I went on a quest to find her
Through the crackling hills
and rolling thunder of Saskatchewan

The wheat swayed in the wind
through the fields
And the road painted a ribbon of grey
Against a sea of yellow
Where the road turned to gravel
It brought me to her

She sounded so wistful and beautiful
I fell in love with her then
I longed to know her
We talked for a moment
But I couldn't tell you what about
Just that I felt euphoria

The drive home was a come down
I knew I had to try to win her heart
So, I wrung the feelings from my veins
In ink on the page

What I wrote I gave to her
And said it was bad poetry
But it was the best I could do
And she deserved so much more
I wish I could have written
a lifetime worth of poems to her

The next time I saw her
She said he chose the ocean over her
I said I knew the ocean
and that he was a fool
I told her I loved her
But not in so many words

That passion that burnt so intensely
Turned to madness
I scared her off

When I finally
awakened from my madness weeks later
She told me I could never see her again

My greatest regret in life
Was losing my grip on reality
If I had been on the deck of Odysseus' ship
And she, a red-haired Siren
I would have gladly drowned
struggling against the sea
To hear one more note

Now I'll never get to know her

Though once in a while

When I listen to her songs

It feels like I do

And once in a while I write her a poem

In the night

With a pen that weeps on the page

In tears that I will forever shed

The passion still burns

Haunting me

Dancing in the night

Near the Ashes: A Saskatchewanian Odessey

The Siren of Saskatchewan

The mermaid knows
A red river flows
Near where the ash trees grow
Winding to the right
Lashes black as night

Skin fair and white
Voice calling through the night
Cutting like a ray of light
Her siren call

I was always fated to fall
I felt it as I drew near
It all become so clear
The rocks below were waiting
But there was never any fear

The Solstice and the Strawberry Moon

Her voice sends shivers in the night

haunted by the longing in her song

Staring at billows of flame

erupting miles away

across a calm expanse

of black night and city light

A river runs through the darkness

Robins and blackbirds dart past

lakes and ponds beside the path

Feeling her presence as she draws near
The full moon strawberry high
and bright in the solstice sky
The sun and his true love
dressed for each other
bright as they could
bright as they ever would
dancing in their day of light

Her melody louder now
come to life
She enters the stage
with faintly freckled fair skin
and messy red hair
flowing down in that Helios light

Oh, does that Sun God favor her
She sang in cooing crescendos
her wistful romantic idealism
whistling through every word

Close Your Eyes

I close my eyes for a moment

And I think of you

Haunting and beautiful

And I slip into a daydream

and I imagine you were mine

And for a moment all the trouble

and the heartache I've known fades away

it doesn't matter anymore

because it brought me to you

And I wish I could tell you why

but I don't know myself

how you move

the rusted and broken gears of my heart

that ground to a halt an age ago

And he wishes he could tell her
how he felt about her
but this is the best he could do

He wishes he could tell her
She's the belle of the ball
in the ballroom of his chest
and how she dances across the floor
turning in circles, and circles in circles
stirring up butterflies and longing sighs
to the music that she made

But the song fades
and my eyes open
and I linger in that moment
but it was just a dream

In Her Absence

The ballroom was bright
The halls were white
Now gone is the light
Now black as the night

Her absence is felt everywhere
Echoes in the silence of loneliness
The floors she used to dance across
Now dusty and bare, wounded by disuse

They long to hear her music again
But he cannot bear the pain to play it
Once he thought his madness was a gift
He curses those moments of inspiration now

He'd give it away to hear her song once more

To watch her dancing though the ballrooms again

To the music that she made

The Harrowing of the Heiros Gamos or As I Fade Away

She destroys me.

No One destroys me.

I destroy me.

Who am I?

No One, am I.

I am No One.

No One, am I?

I am. Am I?

I am…

No One

The Wreckage

She comes in the night
Her face was perfect and bright
Her eyes as auburn as her hair
Sometimes I long to linger there
She wrote and sang

I couldn't help but long
For her lovely siren song
Driven by madness
Crazed by the opposite of sadness
Mind raging in the night

Sanity is a thin shell
And going through mania is hell
Broken and bankrupt
Her nightingale song
Still dancing in the air

Rendered bare

Any chance at love had died there

The pieces of me can't be swept up

I am no-one now I am nowhere

Minerva's Man

The moon rises slowly
over the glassy northern lake
a scene that a black and white
photo would take

Perfectly reflecting her shining face
by morning she is gone without a trace
Her light streaming through the pines
cutting the darkness into lines

I hear her name
here and there
her influence
is everywhere

I always wonder up
at her in the night
hoping for a sign
a glimpse a sight

The goddess of a thousand works
The queen of poetry
she watches over me
Her eyes shining bright
as I write to her in the night
my pen is guided by her light

Prairie Colossus

The grain elevator stands like a colossus
Surrounded by gently swaying wheat
The breeze howling through her bones
Rusted and brittle nails
holding her planks together

The faded paint a distant memory
of when she was bright and new
Echoes of a fading way of life
The last guards' ghost watch has ended

The wheat kings and princes
fade into the past
The prairie princesses
All gone to husbands now
Only ghosts dancing
in the abandoned country halls remain

The rain falling like tears
Shed for our grandparents' dreams
On Monsanto wheat

The Tournament

His lance stuck splintered
And broken in the mud
Only lonely ghosts
With nowhere to go
fill the stands now

His coat lies in tatters
By the turnpike

Stumbling to the stables
The rain beating down
on his muck covered armor
The slippery wet sheen
begins to rust
But the sorrow and salt
of his tears
cannot wash it clean

Home

He lays awake nights longing for her
as the moon longs for the sun on a
silent silver sliver crescent moon night
the memory of her light casting dim shadows
across the darkness

Still, a few rays of her light shine
through so delicately so
sometimes he closes his eyes
for a moment if only to feel
her warmth once again

Sometimes his memory of her
and his hope to somehow see her once more
are all that drive him to stumble

forward in the blizzard
like Odysseus sailing blind into the storm

if home is where the heart is
his heart lived in her
and how he longed to be home again

Your Heart Warms Me

When the light of daybreak
shines upon your radiant face
I wish I could find the words to tell you
what nights together with you mean

How your presence warms
the icy broken shards of my heart
I'd give them to you if I could
but I worry they'd only cut you
as you tried to mend and soften them

Yours so soft and true
As gentle as gentle could be
I hold it in my icy hands
as I try to warm it
but it warms me

Surrender

Every few nights
she visits me
her lovely eyes
bright in the moonlight

Surrendering to her warmth
her fiery auburn hair
draped across my bed
I close my eyes
in her embrace

the words escaping
and breaking
through the cracks
in my heart

I longed to hear
from her in return
the words
she could never say

But then again
she never had to

Manic Depression

My heart raced
110 degrees
she was a fire
the flames raging inside
and I was losing control
it was down to the wire

Up for 7 days no sleep
7 more of this
and she'd make me a liar
I bet I'd marry her
in front of an old town choir

lamenting the love I held for her
or maybe the loss of love to fall
when I heard her longing siren call
especially when the madness set in
I laid it out and gave it my all

Now ghosts of memories
of her whisper by
I wish I could tell her
I never wanted her to see the madness
I guess she'll never really know why

Now I just go about my days
trying not to think of her
most of the time I'm ok
I meet other women here and there
but memories of her are everywhere

She's long gone now
years pass by in a regretful haze
but in my heart she's still ablaze

Shark Week

I was so young
And you a vixen
You showed your world
And that body to me

I wanted you eternally
You promised me
only a moment
While you flashed
your teeth to me
I should have seen
The blood in the water
As I was bleeding

The present turned past
And you were gone
You took my flesh
In a flash
It was that *fast*

First, You Must Love Yourself

Damn that old saying
Why must A man love himself
When He could love her so well
A man need not feel self-love
to truly love her

Somehow she could love me
Even when I will never do that
There are too many
transgressions and failures of character
for me to ever love myself
Any thinking man
Of conscience feels this
Yet I could love her so easily
And be redeemed by her love in turn

Her presence soothes the shame
And she dulls all of the pain
If man is made to suffer
It is upon her breast that
his head is meant to be lain

Drunken Nights

Drunken nights
Under the neon city lights
Friends and amorous lovers
No personas or covers

Drinking deep
Not a thought of sleep
Laughing and sighs
Never claiming to be wise
Feelings expressed by longing stare
No-one writing about nowhere

The wine flows
As the cold Canadian wind blows
and the light glows
hazy in the night's throes

Time slips by
There's a pain that won't die
And sometimes I remember why
broken hearted but too masculine to cry

The Oak and the Ash

Broken bows
The crack of wood
Trees counting years
The rings only show
when it's too late
Bleeding sap

Now look what we've done
The oak and the ash
were so young

Madness Sweet Madness

Drive my pen and inspire my mind
The bipolar highs hang around
my neck like a noose
The gallows floor falls out
and the madness is loose

Dropping onto a bronco
our throats tied together
Every time it bucks the noose tightens
Scarring the muscle of our necks
My hands bleeding from
the rough cutting rope
struggle to hold on

I write in my heart's blood
on the beef of its back
Before the rope slips from my hands
And I'm lying in the mud
As the bronco in its madness
With hooves covered
In blood and bone
tramples me again and again

Wild Albertan Sky

The still of the night lingers
Memories of red and golden
sunlight dancing on the purple thyme
then brilliant orange turned to black

The majesty of an Albertan sky
Not soon forgotten

The coolness sets in
A train whistles past
somewhere
in the darkness

The boxcars thunder and rumble
Graffiti etched onto every one
battle scarred
the veterans roll past

The golden wheat sways
in the chinook wind
Sometimes I picture
someone from the past
Running her fingers through it
Red hair glistening in the sunlight
As she slowly walks
Away from me
In her white dress
Through the fields of grain
And I watch her go

Under a Blue Moon

As a blue moon rises to the east
Wisps of cloud float above the lake
Moonlight reflects in ripples
As Minerva dances on the water
The sun is setting in the west

Another day done
Another day older
As I look into her eyes
Is it a future I see?

She's not what I expected
When I sent up a wish
so earnest long ago
For a partner I could love
With my sanguine heart

I got lost in her tangled locks
And her sweet innocence tied the knots
She's wiser than I know
with a youthful and playful heart

She loves coffee
And ancient books
My heart aches
While she gives me
come hither looks

Never Use the Word Love in a Poem

When the nights light shines
And you're in my arms again
the cruelty of the world fades away
In a serene peace you and I lay
And in my arms I hope you'll stay

When the nights light shines
Young and hauntingly beautiful
You rest your tired eyes
Sweet and innocent but so wise
I lay in repose and can't help but sigh
I smile at my good fortune

When the nights light shines
And the ancient starlight casts shadows
across your sweet and effervescent face
peering down through the window pane
I surrender to your softness I am slain

When the nights light shines
I've let go and for a moment I know no pain
And all the loss I've felt washes away
Like blood in the soothing rain
And I bask in the starlight for a moment
Lingering in it
But the world fades back in
And you're in my arms again
In a serene peace you and I lay
And in my arms I hope you'll stay

Circles in Cycles

The circle of the cycle comes round
Like the planets orbiting the sun
Or the sun orbiting the black hole
at the center of the galaxy
the universe works in circles
And we all end up where we started
Like a yo-yo we stall and hang while we spin
But God flicks his wrist
And we return to his fold
Until it's time for another spin

The Harsh Light of Day

Billows of steam
Blow from its smoke stack
The engine chugs and the gears grind
As the train leaves the station
She looks back for a long moment
Before her handkerchief falls to the palisade
The steam must've gotten into my eyes
As she pulled away from me

I used to look forward to a new day
And the promise it'd bring
Now I hate the harsh light
It takes her away from me again
In my dreams we still dance together
Through the ballrooms in my chest
Stirring up butterflies and longing sighs

But she's long gone now
And that light's gonna come
No matter how tightly I hold her in my arms
That train's always gonna pull away
And I'm always gonna be left there
At that station
With salty steam running down my face
and her last glance in my eyes
As the sun rises

Doing Time in the COVID Hotel

You wish you could tell her
How special she is to you
How your love for her grows
Every day absent her
But the words don't flow
You just hope she knows

Underlying conditions they tell you
You feel giddy and excited
Feeling your mortality
with every breath
And cough
They tell you it's serious
That you should take it seriously
But you just look at them and smile
Only feeling alive
When death stalks you

A life absent struggle or danger
Numb inside from the monotony
Ten days holed up in the COVID hotel
When this is all over will you go back
To a life taken for granted

Only feeling dead inside
Waiting for another virus
to take your breath away
Are you dead inside
Am I dead inside

Prairie Girl

The wind whistles
through the wheat
Her prairie song
pulls at my heart
Memories filled with
the ecstasy of joy
And the ache of grief

Her siren song
echoes through the grain
I can hear it as I walk
through the fields
Hands outstretched
Caressing the wheat
Wishing it were her hair
It tickles my fingers

If only I could feel
her warm embrace
Once more
She knows not
How this exile tortures me
She could drive
a man to madness
And she did once
Long ago

The Tragedy of Our Malady

She's cursed by it too
Memories of the intensity of joy
and the ecstasy of pain
echo in her voice

I know in a moment
of stillness and serenity
She too is afflicted
by the fire inside her

The bipolar blues burn within
the furnace of our hearts
Stoked by love and madness
Crazed when not quenched by sadness
Euphoric in a state of bliss
before our grasp on reality slips

The Icarus heights crash down
Broken wings all mangled and melted
Torn and drugged and dragged away
Cut from our backs in the ambulance bay

Wheeled into the psychiatric ward
Forlorn for a month or more
Where the doctors
don't bother to justify why
You're locked in and drugged so high
The world goes on around you
And all you can do is watch it go by

One day you're released
And left to sweep up the remains
Every circle of the cycle
leaves more wreckage
And less to be salvaged
And one day there's nothing left
The ghost of you disappears
Just whispers in the ether

And the bottle drops to the floor
Or the strand of a rope snaps taut
tied to the balcony iron
Or the hammer clicks
And all those memories of joy and pain
Are just splattered on the wall behind you

The price of these waxen wings is high
They say bipolar takes one in five
That is the tragedy of our malady
Will she die by her own hand?
Will I?

Inevitable as Rain

My love for you

is as inevitable as rain
Flowing to the ocean
Running down your skin
Coursing between your fingers
Flowing down like salty tears
Returning to the sea

My love for you

is as inevitable as the sun
The light of it ever present
In the sunlight and

reflected moon beams
Unintentionally burning

your beautiful skin

My love for you wounds my soul
To a degree you'll never know

In my Haunting Dreams

In my haunting dreams
Dreams of what could have been,
I am a bird
walking down
Roads not taken.
Or stumbled down,
Unnaturally hopping,
Making a mess of things
Like I always do.

In my haunting dreams,
Dreams of my bird wings
Once fast and fierce as a falcon,
Clipped and useless now.
Is this how one gets old?
Admitting defeat, submitting.
Flight forsaken,
Wings bent and broken at the fold.

In my haunting dreams
I'm a pugilist
Who cannot land a punch.
I struggle with my foe,
So many blows do I throw
But his face, my fists will never know.

In my haunting dreams,
I'm a poet
Whose words never flow,
Whose rhymes don't go,
Whose poems are never read,
Whose name is never said.

Sad Songs

They seep into your bones
Wrought with meaning only hinted at
Crafted with emotional hammer blows
That echo in every note she brings to bare

The queen of wistfulness
She crafts the kind of songs
you close your eyes to
She crafts the kind of songs
you lose yourself in
That timeless reverie
It haunts me

You longed for her for years
While life and lovers pass you by
And you think it's romantic
Because your heart breaks
With every song she writes

But those songs aren't about you
And they never will be
There's no romance
in spending your life waiting for her
Only tragedy you can
only blame yourself for

She'll never love you
Like the ones
you've cast aside for her
You'll never love anyone
like you've loved her
Obsession is the cruelest sickness
Of the heart

But you've got to move on
You can't love a shadow any longer
That's all she'll ever be to you

Ithaca

She writes beautiful melodies
And scribbles love notes
In between the lines of ancient tomes
Her soft touch and gentle heart
Can be seen in every pen stroke
And felt in every caress

She sees people for their best
I try to live up to what she senses
I owe her nothing less
I hold no pretenses
Within her presence

We whisper to each other
Songs of love and pain
She knows all my tunes by heart
But sharing with her is not in vain

In her messy apartment
My heart aches for her
In a way I've not known before

Father

Memories echo through the years
Of a gunshot I was too young to hear
A life ended without a second thought
Living is a battle but worthy of being fought

Now as time passes the echo is almost gone
I fight my own battle
it's too early to say I've won
Perhaps you steeled me against the act
But that's just speculation
the damage to my life you caused is fact

The Search for Meaning

Men have found madness
and serenity searching for meaning
The absence of it
is the essence of despair
Much of my life I've found it nowhere

Can it be found in the smell of a lovers hair
Perhaps in a job well done, when the pay is
fair
Or in an old prairie homestead with the cattle
Hearing their cow bells rattle

Perchance it's in a lonely lighthouse
Flowing and coursing
Coming and going
In and out
like the tides

I have no ancient sages wisdom
Meaning can be felt in every moment
or none of them
Found in the slums or the penthouses
Bought with a smile and an embrace
or a money filled briefcase

I've tasted meaning in all these things and places
Sometimes in the smiling remembrance of past lovers faces

All I know is this
These moments of meaning will pass you by
There to be felt and appreciated or denied
Grasp them and drink them in like a sunrise
or let them slide away You decide

The Aviary

An underdog of a bar
On a bad block
You'd never know it was there
Walk past and you'd miss it
But if you listen
On the right night
Music echoes
through its wooden bones

Art lines the walls
An owl headed gunslinger
stares you down
Like one of Hunter S. Thompson's
High powered mutants
Too rare to live
too cool not to buy

It's burned once
But it still stands
Thursday night
They'll test your
brains might
King Quizzard
and the scoreboard wizard
Laying down the questions

Liquor and classical books
reside on the shelves
The proprietors can tell you
And sell you Hemingway's
favorite cocktail

The word hip may come to mind
But that would be selling it short
There's an authenticity to it
And to the people who work there

Dreams

She haunts me in my dreams
Every few months now it seems
When Luna's light is bright
And we're under cover of night

Her ghostly whisper carries
And she dances like nightingale faeries
Across a dreamscape of the prairies

Singing her longing haunting tune
My heart breaks again, I am in ruin

I curse those dreams when I wake
all I wish for the morning will take

Smoldering Auburn

Well her hair was a smoldering auburn
And her skin was white as snow
I'd have given anything to call her my darlin'
But hers was a love I never would know

I longed to look into her hazel eyes
To knock on her door and be let in
And to kiss her lips as red as wine
Oh, to caress her soft blushing skin

In the night she breaks my heart
Then she passes through the wreckage
Dancing amongst the broken pieces
scattered across the ocean tide

Midnight Driver

The piano notes play softly
in the hazy November night
the darkness of the trees
and the neon city lights

The rain drops fall softly
the trees bare and weary
months to go
before the respite of spring

another ring around the circles
years of perseverance
lost limbs and lovers scars
carved into their flesh

street lights turning
yellow and red then green
ghost lights reflecting off
the streets wet empty sheen

No other headlight beams
The midnight drivers dream

Alone, he races against himself
or perhaps against the ghost
of someone he's known

I sit on my own
listening to the
musings of a dead man
what makes a life worth living I ask
I am alone

In the Throes of Thanatos (The Death Instinct)

On a quiet, still night I ponder
The suns long gone down yonder
And here am I left the coast to wander

The love I've known has died
Carried away in the ocean tide
then broken on the rocks of the crimson night
I carry on despite the lack of light
A shadow of a shadow now, I still abide
Perhaps I just lack the mettle for suicide

Less and less survives every loss
Every high water mark pulled back and lost
Every heartache exacting it's cost

In the heart of the darkness,
Thanatos surrounds me
But I am not lost

Burning

Beaten down
Black and blue
After a while the defeat
Gets inside of you

Once the light
inside your eyes
Glistened as you would
Hope to rise

Disappointment and loss
Tear those lights outta your eyes
Those hopes and dreams
Fall apart

That's why
you gotta steel
your own heart
Against the cold world

Can you feel it beat
Can you feel that heat
It breaks like a gunshot
Clean through

But it's up to you
If it shrivels and dies
Or burns harder for the bullet

Through Those Pines

A violin whines

Among the deep green pines

The setting sunlight

Streams through them in lines

I keep walking

This mountain path alone

Thirty-eight and still not grown

Sad and Wishin'

That I was a kind of man

The kind of man you could love

But I'm frozen in the pines

Arrested by a broken heart

Hangin' on a bloody sleeve

His slow hand writes her

A lamentation in the night

Looking up at the moon

And the stars through those pines

The Inverted Tree

Wrecked upon the deep

Lighthouse swings round burning weak

Tide writhing without feelings

He drowned in the desert

Grains of sorrow in his hair

One day there was one

Meaning here and gone

Once there were trees

Upside down on his knees

The bills come due

Waiting for the morning hue

Jack boots shifting the damp sand

Cutting diamonds with coal

Blood and brine toss against the rocks

Rust in his tangled locks

As the hounds envy the fox

As the Starlight Fades

In the future
we'll live thousands of years
Not our descendants but you and I
We'll be superheroes
with no one to save
No injustices to fight against
no inequity to strive against

Nano robots will flow from our veins
Keeping us young forever
Immortal Philosopher
kings and queens
Warrior poets roaming the stars
Colonizing new worlds
Propagating the species
Effortlessly stronger and faster
than the heroes in stories of old

We'll find our ideal lovers
Or maybe design them
And live a thousand lifetimes
with anyone we choose
Countless worlds filled to the brim
with our children

One day we may grow weary
And long to leave this world behind
And perhaps we'd float hand in hand
across the event horizon
of a supermassive black hole
Into the great beyond
Conquistadors of death
In search of the last frontier

But at the end of time
As the last starlight fades
As heat death takes hold
When the last human
has forgotten his own name
When the sandcastles we built
Are all washed away
by the ocean tides of time

Will it matter
how vigorously we lived
Or how passionately we loved
When there's no one
left to experience
The beauty we created
Or the music that we made

Let Go

Let go of the worry,
let go of everything,
just let it flow,
I'm talking to it
and it loves us all equally,
there is no judgement,
just be.

All souls are equal,
no matter what they've done
or what's been done to them,
how much they've needed
or how much they've given,
we are all loved equally,
and so much,
it knows everything about us
and loves us all the same

The Moon and the Ocean Tide

You were the moon
and I the ocean tide
ever chasing after you
ever bathed in your
bright beacon light
the beauty of your face
reflected upon the water

Spinning in circles
and circles in circles
waxing and waning
teasing me with glimpses
of your sensual curved form

I would meet you there
Where the setting moon sets
but I just crash upon the rocks
I couldn't even tell you where
because you were never
even really there

Printed in Great Britain
by Amazon

d0ac6daa-d51b-4733-bec0-18886635af8bR01